CHRISTMAS Comes to BETHLEHEM
Coloring Book

Written by: Robin Fogle
Illustrated by: Christian Elden

© 2012 Warner Press, Inc
All rights reserved   Made in the USA

The purchase of this reproducible activity book grants you the rights to photocopy the contents for classroom use.
Notice: It is unlawful to copy these pages for resale purposes. Copy permission is for private use only.

Warner Press Kids
educate • nurture • inspire
www.warnerpress.org

30580029313

Bethlehem was a small town, nestled in the hills of Judea.

Usually the town was quiet, but today it was alive with activity! Strangers hurried among the townspeople, crowding the marketplace and side streets.

They were eager to buy food and find lodgings before night.

No one noticed the tired and travel-stained young couple, entering the city gate. Like so many others, they had come to Bethlehem for the census, to be counted according to Caesar Augustus' command.

The trip had been especially hard for the young woman, Mary. She was expecting a baby any day. How she wished for a nice place to lie down and rest! Joseph asked for a room at the inn, but the innkeeper said, "We have no rooms left."

When the innkeeper saw Mary, he had an idea.
"Would you like to sleep in my stable? I know it's not much, but you would be safe and warm for the night."
Joseph knew Mary could not go much farther.
"Thank you for your kindness," he said.

© 2012 Warner Press, Inc All rights reserved

Joseph piled up some soft, clean straw to make a bed for Mary. Before long, a new sound came from the stable—not the quiet moo of a cow or baa of a sheep, but the sweet little cry of a baby!

© 2012 Warner Press, Inc All rights reserved

As Mary held her baby, she remembered the words of the angel, many months before: "You will give birth to a Son and will name Him Jesus." Mary's baby was extra special because He was God's only Son. Carefully, she wrapped Him in soft cloths and laid Him in a manger to sleep.

While Mary and Joseph watched over Baby Jesus, some shepherds were watching over their sheep in the fields outside of Bethlehem.

© 2012 Warner Press, Inc All rights reserved

Suddenly an angel appeared in the night sky! "Don't be afraid," the angel said. "I have good news! Today your Savior has been born!" Then the sky was filled with angels praising God. "Glory to God in the highest!" they said.

The shepherds said, "Hurry! Let's go to Bethlehem to see Jesus." They found Him just as the angels said they would. The shepherds were so happy they told everyone they met about Jesus!

Some time later, wise men came from a land far away in the east. They had seen a special star in the night sky and knew it meant something important had happened.

They went to King Herod and asked, "Where is the one who is born king of the Jews? We have come to worship Him." The king said, "I don't know, but when you find Him, tell me where He is and I will worship Him too."

© 2012 Warner Press, Inc All rights reserved

The wise men followed the star on and on. At last it stopped above the house where Jesus was.

© 2012 Warner Press, Inc All rights reserved

The wise men worshiped Jesus and gave Him gifts of gold, frankincense and myrrh. Then they went home by a different road because God had warned them in a dream not to tell King Herod where Jesus was.

Just like Christmas came to Bethlehem when God sent Jesus to earth, Christmas can come to us when we ask Jesus to stay forever in our hearts. That's the way to celebrate Christmas every day!

© 2012 Warner Press, Inc All rights reserved